Who Was
Muhammad Ali?

Who Is Muhammad Ali?

by James Buckley Jr.

illustrated by Stephen Marchesi

Penguin Workshop

To Conor and Katie: Think of Ali when you need
courage of your convictions—JB

PENGUIN WORKSHOP
An Imprint of Penguin Random House LLC, New York

Text copyright © 2014, 2016 by James Buckley Jr. Illustrations copyright © 2014 by
Stephen Marchesi. Cover illustration copyright © 2014 by Penguin Random House LLC.
All rights reserved. Published in 2014 as *Who Is Muhammad Ali?* and in 2016 as *Who Was
Muhammad Ali?* by Grosset and Dunlap, an imprint of Penguin Random House LLC.
This edition published in 2019 by Penguin Workshop, an imprint of Penguin Random
House LLC, New York. PENGUIN and PENGUIN WORKSHOP are trademarks of
Penguin Books Ltd. WHO HQ & Design is a registered trademark of
Penguin Random House LLC. Printed in the USA.

Visit us online at www.penguinrandomhouse.com.

The Library of Congress has catalogued *Who Is Muhammad Ali?* under Control Number:
20144944568

ISBN 9780448479552   20 19 18

Contents

Who Was
Muhammad Ali?

Cassius Clay liked to shock people. He was a boxer who liked to brag about how great he was. He liked to show off to get attention and sometimes spoke in poetic rhymes. And he liked to win.

But he was only twenty-two years old. He had never fought for the world heavyweight championship—the most coveted title in boxing. He was considered to be fast, but not quite tough enough.

Sonny Liston was the champion. He had held on to his championship title for nearly two years. He was powerful, experienced, hard-hitting, and fierce. Many other boxers were afraid to get into the ring with him.

On February 25, 1964, a boxing match took place in Miami Beach, Florida, between the "Louisville Lip"—as Clay was known—and the powerful champ, Liston.

Once the fight began, Liston tried to overpower Clay. But Cassius moved quickly and danced away from the big man's punches. As the rounds went by, thirty-two-year-old Sonny Liston grew tired. His legs felt heavy. Clay, meanwhile, continued to move with grace and speed, darting in to hit Liston again and again.

After six rounds, Liston was worn out. He could not come out to meet Clay for the seventh round. The fight was over! Cassius Clay had won!

Clay erupted from his own corner and leaped onto the ropes around the ring. "I shook up the world!" he shouted as people filled the ring to celebrate. "I shook up the world!" By defeating Sonny Liston, Clay became the heavyweight boxing champion of the world.

Soon after, Cassius Clay shocked his family and the world again when he changed his religion from Christianity to Islam, and his name to Muhammad Ali.

As the years went by, Ali would be a champion time and again. He would go on to surprise people, both in and out of the ring. Through it all, he would show the same unique style and courage he had shown in 1964. After his big win against Sonny Liston, he yelled out to the crowd, "I am the greatest!"

In the years that followed, he proved it.

Chapter 1
Life in Louisville

He became world famous with the name Muhammad Ali, but he was born Cassius Marcellus Clay Jr. on January 17, 1942, in Louisville, Kentucky.

"We called him 'GG' when he was born," said his mother, Odessa Clay. "He used to say 'gee, gee, gee, gee.'" She said that Cassius was running and talking before most other babies. And he

was strong. He accidentally hit his mother in the mouth once, loosening one of her teeth.

In 1944, Cassius's brother, Rudolph, was born. Cassius looked out for his baby brother, and he would sometimes even try to stop his mom from spanking Rudolph, who was also known as Rudy.

Their mother raised them as Christian, attending a Baptist church. "Every Sunday, she dressed me up, took me and my brother to church, and taught us the way she thought was right," Cassius said later in his life.

When the boys were a bit older, their father, also named Cassius, would bring them along on his job painting signs. When they weren't working with their dad or at school, the boys played together. They loved playing marbles and touch football. Cassius was a very fast runner. He would sometimes race the school bus, running alongside as his friends cheered him on.

Together the two boys were full of energy.
Friends called them the "Wrecking Crew," since
something always seemed to break when they were
around. Cassius was very outgoing, happy to laugh
and talk with anyone. "By the time he was four, he
had all the confidence in the world," his mother
remembered. The brothers could find plenty to
do in their own neighborhood, but they knew not
to go to certain parts of Louisville. In America
in the 1940s and 1950s, especially in the South,

black and white people often did not mix. Many white people felt that blacks should be separate from whites. Southern states like Kentucky even had laws that said black people could not swim in public pools or go to school with white children. Cassius grew up in a divided America, and it was something he never forgot.

In 1954, when Cassius was twelve years old, he and his friends rode their bikes to Louisville's Columbia Auditorium to see the Louisville Home Show.

THE FIRST CASSIUS M. CLAY

THE FIRST CASSIUS MARCELLUS CLAY WAS A WHITE MAN BORN IN 1810 IN KENTUCKY. THOUGH HIS FATHER OWNED SLAVES, YOUNG CLAY WAS AGAINST SLAVERY. WHEN HE GREW UP, HE SPOKE

OUT AGAINST IT. HE PUBLISHED AN ANTI-SLAVERY NEWSPAPER CALLED THE *TRUE AMERICAN*.

HIS VIEWS WERE VERY UNPOPULAR IN THE SOUTH. HE WAS ATTACKED BY MOBS AND HIS FAMILY SUFFERED.

CLAY WORKED TO GET ABRAHAM LINCOLN ELECTED PRESIDENT IN 1860, AND DURING THE CIVIL WAR, HE LED A GROUP OF VOLUNTEER SOLDIERS WHO FOUGHT TO DEFEND WASHINGTON, DC. DURING AND AFTER THE WAR, HE SERVED AS AMERICA'S MINISTER TO RUSSIA. AFTER RETURNING TO THE UNITED STATES, HE WORKED FOR THE REPUBLICAN PARTY FOR MANY YEARS BEFORE HE DIED IN 1903.

CLAY'S ANTI-SLAVERY VIEWS INSPIRED A BLACK FAMILY TO NAME THEIR SON AFTER HIM IN 1912. IN 1942, THAT MAN, CASSIUS CLAY SR., NAMED HIS SON CASSIUS CLAY JR.

In addition to furniture and appliance displays, the boys also found such delights as free popcorn. After they had wandered around the show for several hours, Cassius found that his bike, a beloved red-and-white Schwinn, had been stolen.

He was very upset. Someone said that a policeman was in the building, so Cassius went to report the theft. Cassius was crying. He said that he would like to hit whoever stole his bike.

Joe Martin, the policeman, was actually teaching a boxing class in the basement gym of the auditorium. He invited Cassius to try boxing in order to channel his anger with some degree of control. Cassius soon discovered that not only did he enjoy boxing, he was really good at it.

Not long after he began to train with Joe Martin, Cassius was featured on a local TV show called *Tomorrow's Champions*.

Cassius, who was still only twelve years old, took to the ring against a youngster named

Ronnie O'Keefe. Cassius won the fight, and that started his amazing boxing career.

Cassius never did recover his stolen bike. From then on, he put all his energy into boxing. Martin had to open the gym at 4:00 a.m. some days to let Cassius in to train before school. Cassius wore heavy steel-toed boots to develop his leg muscles as he ran. He drank energy shakes and raw eggs to build up his strength. He never drank soda, but instead drank water mixed with garlic. It didn't smell good, but it made him feel good! In the ring, he learned to use his speed. He found that he could avoid many punches by leaning back quickly and that his hands could move as fast as his feet. As he won more and more fights, he was not shy about telling people about how good he was.

He paid more attention to boxing than he did to his schoolwork. But he felt that his destiny was in the ring. As early as his high-school years,

he was boasting that he would be "the greatest of all time." Even his principal joked that he would send school troublemakers to Cassius for him to deal with!

He was not tough through and through, however. Though he loved to be the center of attention, Cassius was very shy around girls. In fact, he fainted the first time he kissed a girl after a date!

By the time he was eighteen, Cassius had won 100 of his 108 amateur fights. He and Martin had to travel to many cities for boxing matches. In most of them, Cassius saw the separation between black and white people. African American boxers had to carefully choose which restaurants they went to. They could stay only at certain hotels that allowed black people. Cassius took all this in and remembered it.

The young fighter truly believed he would be a champion. In 1957, he looked up the famous boxing trainer Angelo Dundee. Dundee was in Louisville at the time, working with another fighter. Cassius called Dundee at his hotel and asked

ANGELO DUNDEE

to meet him. The brash young man said, "I'm gonna win the Golden Gloves, and I'm gonna win the Olympics in 1960, and I want to talk to you." Dundee did not believe the young man could win a national amateur tournament like the Golden Gloves, so he did not agree to train him. He did not realize that one day Clay's prediction would come true.

THE SPORT OF BOXING

BOXING HAS BEEN A SPORT FOR THOUSANDS OF YEARS. ANCIENT GREEKS INCLUDED BOXING IN THEIR OLYMPIC GAMES. UNTIL THE 1800S MEN BOXED WITHOUT GLOVES, USING THEIR BARE FISTS.

BUT IN 1867 A SERIES OF RULES WERE CREATED TO MAKE BOXING SAFER. TODAY'S BOXING IS BASED ON THOSE RULES.

A BOXING MATCH PITS TWO PEOPLE OF NEARLY EQUAL WEIGHT AGAINST EACH OTHER IN THE BOXING RING. WEIGHT CLASSES RANGE FROM STRAWWEIGHT (105 POUNDS), THROUGH

WELTERWEIGHT (147 POUNDS), AND UP TO HEAVY-WEIGHT (200 POUNDS AND UP).

EACH MATCH IS A SET NUMBER OF THREE-MINUTE ROUNDS. OLYMPIC FIGHTS LAST THREE ROUNDS, WHILE HEAVYWEIGHT PROFESSIONAL FIGHTS CAN BE AS MANY AS FIFTEEN. THE FIGHTERS GET A ONE-MINUTE BREAK BETWEEN EACH ROUND. A REFEREE IS IN THE RING WITH THE BOXERS.

IF ONE FIGHTER IS KNOCKED DOWN AND THE REFEREE COUNTS TO TEN, THE FIGHT IS OVER BY KNOCKOUT. IF A FIGHTER IS SO HURT HE CAN'T CONTINUE, THE WINNER EARNS A TECHNICAL KNOCKOUT (TKO). IF THE FIGHT "GOES THE DISTANCE" (FINISHES ALL ROUNDS), THREE JUDGES CHOOSE WHO WON BASED ON SCORES KEPT DURING THE FIGHT.

In 1959 and 1960, Cassius won his first big titles. He was the winner of both the Golden Gloves and the Amateur Athletic Union championships in both of those years. The next step up the boxing ladder was a big one: the Summer Olympics.

The 1960 Olympic trials determined which boxers would be on the team to represent the United States. Cassius fought several tough bouts . . . and he won them all! He was named to the US team that was headed to Rome, Italy.

Chapter 2
Olympic Champ

Going to Rome meant that Cassius would have to fly. There was one problem: The powerful boxer was afraid to fly! Joe Martin worked hard to convince his young student to fly to Rome. Cassius did not take chances, however. He bought a parachute to wear on the airplane!

After arriving safely, he soon became a familiar sight among the world's athletes. The energetic young man was thrilled to see everyone. Staying in the Olympic Village in Rome, he visited with athletes from dozens of countries. He wanted to meet everyone he could, mostly to talk about himself.

Talking was something that Cassius was very good at. Even as a teenage boxer, he had not been afraid to boast about his skills. This was very different than many athletes, and certainly black athletes. Some white American fans did not appreciate black people who spoke up or spoke out. Cassius didn't care. He was loud, funny, and proud.

Cassius liked to brag and he liked to box. He battled men from Belgium, Russia, and Australia. Each was a difficult fight, but Cassius won them all. He had a unique way of expressing himself and he had a unique style in the ring. Unlike many fighters, he danced, shuffled, and moved around. Most fighters stood their ground and tried to overpower their opponents. Cassius could hit, but he was very good at avoiding hits, too. He seemed to be playing a role or acting out a certain part . . . until his powerful fists connected with big punches.

His final Olympic match, for the light-heavyweight gold medal (for fighters up to 178 pounds), was his toughest yet. Cassius faced Zbigniew Pietrzykowski from Poland, who had been champion of Europe three times and had fought in the 1956 Olympics. The Polish fighter was older, bigger, and stronger.

The first two rounds were about even. In
the third round, Cassius gave the Polish boxer a
bloody nose and landed many blows. When the
judges scored the fight, Cassius was named the
winner. The kid from Louisville had earned an
Olympic gold medal!

Clay returned to the United States, still talking and still wearing his gold medal. He toured New York City, shaking hands with everyone he met. Then he returned to a "welcome home" event in Louisville.

At the ceremony in Louisville, he read a poem he had written. Such poems would become a well-known part of his personal style.

To make America the greatest is my goal,
So I beat the Russian, and I beat the Pole.

Not everyone in town was so excited by his success. Even in 1960, some people still were not happy to see a black person getting so much attention. Cassius had represented America in Rome, but he said that even though he had a gold medal, some people were still calling him *boy*. That word was a great insult to a black man.

Cassius did not let such prejudice slow him down. He knew that his next big step was to become a professional. To this point, as an amateur, he had not been paid for any of his fights. He had to be an amateur to fight in the Olympics. But with the Games behind him, it was time to move up. He wanted to buy a car for his parents and to help Rudy, who was also training to be a boxer. Boxing can be expensive. A fighter has to hire trainers and assistants, rent gyms, and travel to fights. He only gets paid when he fights. To get the money he needed, Cassius signed a deal with a group of businessmen. They agreed to pay for his training for five years in return for a percentage of all the money he won. They also gave him a bonus just for signing with them.

One of the first things Cassius did with that money was to hire Angelo Dundee to be his trainer. Dundee remembered meeting Cassius back in Louisville. He had watched the young fighter's progress and thought he could help him become a better boxer. After his Olympic success, Cassius had a new goal: to be heavyweight champion of the world. He knew he needed Dundee's help.

Another thing Cassius did with the bonus was buy his parents a new pink Cadillac.

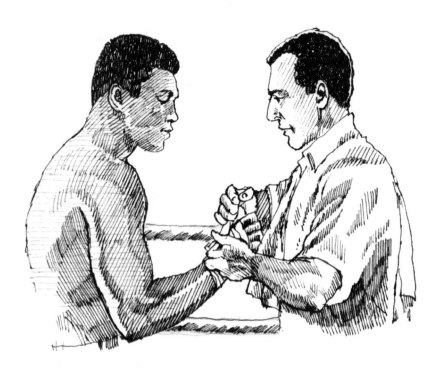

In 1960, when he was eighteen years old, Cassius moved to Miami, where Dundee ran a gym. With this support, Cassius went from amateur to professional and kept winning just as he always had.

He kept talking, too. Though he was new to professional boxing, he boasted that he would win every bout. He started predicting how many rounds the fight would last . . . and he was usually right. He said this before a 1963 match with Doug Jones:

Jones like to mix,
So I'll let it go six.
If he talks jive,
I'll cut it to five.
And if he talks some more,
I'll cut it to four!

Clay's loud, fast talk and bragging earned him a new nickname: the Louisville Lip. But he knew about an old saying in sports: It's not bragging if you can back it up.

Chapter 3
King of the World!

For the next several years, Cassius trained full time in Miami with Dundee. He also kept winning. Cassius won eight fights in 1961 and six in 1962. He didn't lose one fight. All the while, his trainer was impressed by how hard Cassius worked, just as Joe Martin had been.

During some of his rare time away from the training gym, Cassius became friends with Sam Saxon, who was part of the Nation of Islam.

"I was training for a fight," Ali said, "and met a follower of Elijah Muhammad named Captain Sam. He invited me

SAM SAXON

to a meeting and after that, my life changed."

Elijah Muhammad was the leader of the
Nation of Islam. This religious movement was for
black Americans only. It believed that black and
white people should be separate. Its members also
followed some of the beliefs of Islam, an ancient
religion that started in the Middle East. People
who follow Islam are called Muslims.

NATION OF ISLAM

ISLAM IS A RELIGION THAT WAS REVEALED TO THE PROPHET MUHAMMAD IN THE SEVENTH CENTURY IN WHAT IS NOW SAUDI ARABIA. PEOPLE WHO BELIEVE IN ISLAM ARE CALLED MUSLIMS. THE FAITH SPREAD RAPIDLY IN THE MIDDLE EAST, AFRICA, AND ASIA. TODAY MORE THAN 1.5 BILLION PEOPLE AROUND THE WORLD FOLLOW ISLAM.

THE NATION OF ISLAM (NOI) IS DIFFERENT. IT WAS FOUNDED BY WALLACE D. FARD IN DETROIT IN 1930. FARD DISAPPEARED IN 1934 AND A MAN WHO CALLED HIMSELF ELIJAH MUHAMMAD TOOK OVER LEADERSHIP OF THE GROUP.

MANY OF THE BELIEFS OF THE NATION OF ISLAM MIRROR THOSE OF OTHER MUSLIMS, SUCH AS CALLING GOD "ALLAH," PRAYING FIVE TIMES A DAY, AND NOT EATING PORK OR DRINKING ALCOHOL.

ELIJAH MUHAMMAD

FARD AND MUHAMMAD ADDED OTHER IDEAS. THEY TAUGHT THAT BLACK PEOPLE ARE ALL DESCENDED FROM ANOTHER, EARLIER RACE THAT HAD BEEN SPLIT APART BY WHITE PEOPLE. ELIJAH MUHAMMAD TOLD HIS FOLLOWERS THAT WHITE PEOPLE WERE THE ENEMY. THIS MADE HIM UNPOPULAR NOT ONLY WITH WHITES, BUT WITH BLACKS WHO WERE WORKING FOR EQUALITY.

ELIJAH MUHAMMAD DIED IN 1975. HIS SON WARITH DEEN TOOK HIS PLACE AS THE LEADER OF THE NATION OF ISLAM AND SOFTENED MANY OF ITS VIEWS. HE CHANGED THE GROUP'S NAME TO THE AL-ISLAM IN THE WEST. TODAY, A DIFFERENT GROUP, NOT CONNECTED TO WARITH DEEN MOHAMMED, USES THE NAME NATION OF ISLAM.

Cassius talked with Sam Saxon and visited a mosque, which is an Islamic temple. Cassius had heard of the movement before. In high school, he had actually wanted to write an essay in English class about black Muslims, but the teacher would not let him. As Cassius listened at the mosque, he thought about what he heard and became more interested.

Meanwhile, Cassius moved up the heavyweight rankings. From 1960 through 1963, he fought nineteen times and won every fight, most by knockout. His swaggering charm got him as much attention as his great fighting skills. He knew that getting attention in the press would bring more people to the fights. And more people in the audience meant that he would earn more money.

Before each fight, he would entertain reporters and photographers, clowning and joking and showing off. Some writers and boxing fans didn't like how he was acting. Others thought he was fun to watch. He didn't care, as long as they were paying attention.

One of his inspirations was a professional wrestler called Gorgeous George. Like Cassius, George bragged often and loudly. He wore wild costumes, had long, curly blond hair, and made outrageous claims. Cassius once met George before a fight in Las Vegas. The wrestler advised him to keep talking: Make it an act and the people will come.

Cassius traveled to London to fight the great British champion Henry Cooper. He entertained the English press with his wild ways and taunts. He predicted he would beat Cooper in five rounds . . . and he did.

GORGEOUS GEORGE

NOT MANY ATHLETES HAVE CHANGED THE WORLD OF SPORTS, BUT GEORGE WAGNER CERTAINLY DID. BEFORE GEORGE, ATHLETES WERE NOT LOUD, COLORFUL, CONTROVERSIAL, OR FLASHY. AFTER GEORGE, ATHLETES, STARTING WITH MUHAMMAD ALI, KNEW THAT MAKING HEADLINES AND ATTRACTING ATTENTION COULD HELP MAKE THEM FAMOUS—AND MAYBE EVEN MAKE THEM RICH.

WAGNER WAS A WRESTLER IN THE 1940S AND 1950S. HE GAVE HIMSELF NICKNAMES SUCH AS THE "SENSATION OF THE NATION" AND—MOST FAMOUSLY—"GORGEOUS GEORGE." HE DYED HIS HAIR BLOND AND WORE IT IN LONG CURLS. HE WORE COLORFUL CAPES AND BOOTS. BEAUTIFUL MUSIC FILLED THE ARENA AS HE ARRIVED. AN ATTENDANT SPRAYED PERFUME IN THE RING AS WAGNER ENTERED, AND CARRIED A SILVER MIRROR. WRESTLING WAS ONE OF THE FIRST SPORTS TO BECOME POPULAR ON TELEVISION, AND GORGEOUS GEORGE BECAME THE MOST FAMOUS PROFESSIONAL WRESTLER OF HIS TIME

BECAUSE OF THE WAY HE ENTERTAINED THE CROWDS OUTSIDE, AS WELL AS INSIDE, THE RING.

HIS INFLUENCE ON SPORTS AND POPULAR CULTURE CONTINUES TO THIS DAY.

But underneath all the fun, Cassius still had a burning desire to be the champ. Finally, just one man stood in his way: Sonny Liston, who was then the world heavyweight champion.

As good as Cassius was, most boxing experts thought Liston was much better. Liston had already beaten all the other top fighters. He had one of the most powerful punches ever, and he was fearless in the ring. Cassius turned on his attention-getting skills. He called the champ "a big, ugly bear."

SONNY LISTON

He parked a bus in front of Liston's home in Denver. The bus had a sign painted by Cassius's father. It said, *Liston Must Go in Eight*, meaning eight rounds. At the weigh-in before the fight, Cassius pretended to be scared

of Liston. "If he stands and fights, I'll kill him," Liston said.

The fight between Cassius and Sonny Liston was finally held in Miami on February 25, 1964. Even though almost no one thought Clay could win, he danced and moved and avoided the bigger man's punches. The sixth round ended, and Cassius danced back to his corner. He felt great and Liston was breathing hard.

Liston was in pain, and he did not come out for the seventh round. The fight was over! Cassius Clay had done what he always said he would do. He was the heavyweight world champion! As he received his championship belt, fans knew they had seen one of the biggest upsets in the history of boxing. To the new champ, however, his victory was no surprise.

Cassius leaped around the ring. He climbed the ropes and shook his fists in the air. "I am the greatest of *aaaaall* time! I'm the king of the world!"

Chapter 4
Cassius Becomes Muhammad

Not long after his big win over Sonny Liston, Cassius surprised everyone again. He announced that he had joined the Nation of Islam. He said that from then on, his name would be Muhammad Ali. Many people who become Muslims change their names to reflect their new beliefs. The man born as Cassius Clay took a name that means "one worthy of praise." He said that Clay was his "slave name," given to his family by a white man years ago.

Boxing fans had been shocked by Ali's win over Liston, but more people were shocked by this even bigger news. Most fans were very upset. They had supported the young champ, and now they felt that Ali was rejecting them.

By joining a group that was seen as anti-American and anti-Christian, Ali angered many white fans. In fact, for years after his announcement, newspapers and reporters refused to use Ali's new name.

They continued to call him Cassius Clay.

America was very divided over the issue of equal rights for black Americans. Black Americans and many white Americans wanted everyone to have equal rights. However, the Nation of Islam did not call for equal rights. It called for a complete separation of blacks and whites. Ali began to speak out about the NOI's ideas, and this angered many people.

"Jesus was white, Santa Claus was white, Tarzan the king of the jungle was white, everything seems to be white," he said. "Angel food cake is white and devil's food cake is dark. But now that we have a man in America like [NOI leader] Elijah Muhammad, we are the greatest." Ali's brother, Rudy, joined the NOI, too. He changed his name to Rahman Ali. Their parents were upset about the news. Cassius Sr.

and Odessa had raised their sons in the Baptist Church. Ali's father felt that Nation of Islam members were controlling his sons' lives. Odessa Clay was sad that her sons had changed their faith.

Though millions of people, including his family, disagreed with him, Muhammad Ali stuck to his beliefs.

Chapter 5
Taking a Stand

In May 1964, when he was just twenty-two years old, Ali traveled to Africa for the first time and visited Nigeria, Ghana, and Egypt. He met with the leaders of those countries. In Egypt, he rode a camel and visited the pyramids. In Nigeria, he was cheered by enormous crowds. It was an eye-opening trip for the young man.

In Africa, Ali was embraced. He was welcomed as a hero, both for his boxing and his beliefs. Many people in Africa were Muslim, too.

When he got back from Africa, Ali began to look more closely at life in America. He saw the differences between America and Africa. In the African nations he visited, he saw that black people were in charge of countries and not treated like second-class citizens.

"Me being the heavyweight champion feels very small and cheap," he said, "when [I see] how millions of my poor black brothers and sisters are having to struggle just to get human rights in America."

Not long after he came back, he met Sonji Roi, a young woman from Chicago. Though Sonji was

not part of the Nation of Islam, he married her in August 1964. But their marriage was not steady. Sonji did not agree with the NOI people who were influencing Ali.

Ali kept boxing, winning again and again. He won fights in Canada, England, and Germany, along with several in the United States. With every win, his fame grew. He continued making up poems, talking loud, and attracting attention. This was one of his most famous poems:

Float like a butterfly, sting like a bee
His hands can't hit what his eyes can't see

Muhammad Ali carefully planned his poetic way of speaking and his showy style of giving interviews. Journalists and reporters loved to write stories about him.

"Them newspaper people couldn't have been working no better for me if I had been paying them," he said.

Very soon, however, their stories would be working against him.

In the 1960s, young American men were drafted to serve in the military. If a person was drafted, service in the army was not voluntary. It was mandatory. In 1964, Ali had taken a written test for the army, but he had not passed.

In 1966, the army changed its standards. This time, Ali passed. He asked that the army not call him to go to war. He said that he did not support the war the United States was fighting in Vietnam, a small country in Southeast Asia.

Ali based his reasons on his religious beliefs. And he didn't believe that he should have to fight a war against people he did not know. His decision was also a reaction to the ongoing civil rights struggle in America.

During this time, his short marriage to Sonji ended in divorce. A year later, he was drafted into the army and told to report for duty.

On April 28, 1967, he reported to the United States Armed Forces Examining and Entrance Station in Houston. When his name was called he refused to step forward and acknowledge it. Refusing to join the army was against the law. Muhammad Ali was arrested.

VIETNAM WAR

IN 1954, A CIVIL WAR STARTED IN THE FRENCH COLONY OF VIETNAM. THE VIETCONG, A GROUP FROM THE NORTH OF THE COUNTRY, WANTED THE NATION TO BECOME COMMUNIST. THE GOVERNMENT'S MILITARY FOUGHT TO STOP THEM. FRENCH SOLDIERS HELPED THE GOVERNMENT UNTIL THE MID-1950S, WHEN AMERICAN SOLDIERS ARRIVED TO HELP, TOO. VIETNAM SPLIT INTO THE NORTH, CONTROLLED BY THE VIETCONG, AND THE SOUTH, WHICH WAS ANTI-COMMUNIST.

VIETNAM

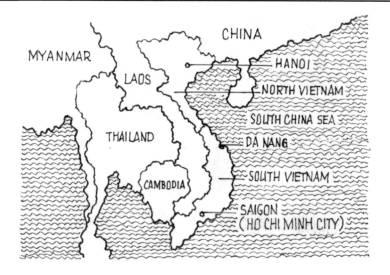

AS THE WAR WENT ON, MORE AND MORE
AMERICAN TROOPS ARRIVED TO HELP SOUTH
VIETNAM. MANY AMERICANS DID NOT AGREE THAT
AMERICA SHOULD BE FIGHTING IN THIS WAR. AS
THE 1960S WENT ON, MORE AND MORE PEOPLE
PROTESTED AGAINST THE WAR. MEANWHILE, 58,000
US SOLDIERS AND PERHAPS AS MANY AS THREE
MILLION VIETNAMESE WERE KILLED.

IN 1975, THE SOUTH VIETNAMESE CAPITAL
OF SAIGON CAME UNDER THE CONTROL OF THE
VIETCONG. NORTH AND SOUTH VIETNAM WERE
REUNITED INTO THE COMMUNIST NATION OF
VIETNAM AND US TROOPS LEFT. MANY AMERICANS
STILL BELIEVE IT WAS A MISTAKE TO HAVE ENTERED
THE WAR AT ALL.

The boxing world was very angry. The groups
that organized the world rankings took away his
heavyweight title, even though Ali had not lost in
the ring. In court, Muhammad Ali was convicted
of draft evasion and sentenced to five years in jail.

Ali's mother had wanted him to join the army.

She had attended all of his important fights and remained close to her son. But she disagreed with his decision.

The great baseball pioneer Jackie Robinson said, "How can he expect to make millions of dollars in this country and then refuse to fight for it?"

After his conviction, while his case was appealed to other courts, Ali remained free. But he could not box. Although the champion was undefeated in twenty-nine professional fights and made millions of dollars a year, he could no longer do his job. Even so, Ali was content.

"I believed in what I was doing," he wrote later. "So no matter what the government did to me, it wasn't a loss."

He said, "If I thought going to war would bring freedom, justice, and equality to twenty-two million Negroes, I'd join tomorrow."

Surprisingly, his spiritual leader, Elijah Muhammad, did not support Ali's decision. Elijah

believed that Ali was glorifying himself and not the Nation of Islam. He was worried that Ali's fame was overshadowing the Nation of Islam and Elijah Muhammad's influence. Also, since joining the NOI, Ali had softened his feelings about white people. Dundee, for example, was his great friend and he was white. The Louisville men who had sponsored him early in his career were white. Eventually, Elijah Muhammad said that Ali was not part of the NOI.

That did not stop Ali from being a Muslim, however. Nor did he ever regret his refusal to be drafted. As a result, for the next three years, the greatest fighter in the world didn't fight— he talked. Ali made hundreds of speeches and appearances, mostly at colleges. He talked about his decision not to join the army. He spoke about Islam and about the Vietnam War. He loved to meet people, anyplace he could.

Ali remarried in 1967. His new wife was Belinda Boyd, who changed her name to Khalilah Ali after they were married. He had first met Belinda in 1961 during a visit to her Islamic grammar school.

She interviewed him for her school paper. He saw her again five years later at a meeting of Nation of Islam believers. They began to stay in touch and when she turned seventeen, Ali was single again. "He just said, 'You're gonna be my wife,'" she remembered. "I said, 'Right.' And that was it . . . He was my first love."

The couple had four children in the next few years: Maryum, twins Jamillah and Rasheda, and Muhammad Ali Jr.

During this time, Ali remained free while his case was appealed to higher courts. Though he did not fight in the ring, Ali was winning. By the late 1960s, more and more people came to agree with him that the Vietnam War was wrong. Millions of people marched and protested. It was a very difficult time in America.

In 1970, Ali was finally granted a license to fight in Georgia. A year later, the US Supreme Court would say that his conviction had been wrong. He was free. Ali's next goal was to reclaim the heavyweight championship.

Chapter 6
Two Huge Fights

While Ali was banned from boxing, a new heavyweight champion arose. "Smokin'" Joe Frazier had one of the most powerful punches ever. He never seemed to mind getting hit, either.

Muhammad Ali had become world famous during his time away from the ring, but he remained controversial even after returning to boxing. Some fans still resented his choices, while others loved him even more for standing up for what he thought was right. Everyone agreed on one thing, however: They were all eager to see him fight Joe Frazier. After his time off, would Ali still be a great boxer?

The match was scheduled for March 8, 1971, in Madison Square Garden in New York City. Every one of the more than

20,000 seats in the Garden was sold out. Three hundred million people around the world watched the Fight of the Century on television.

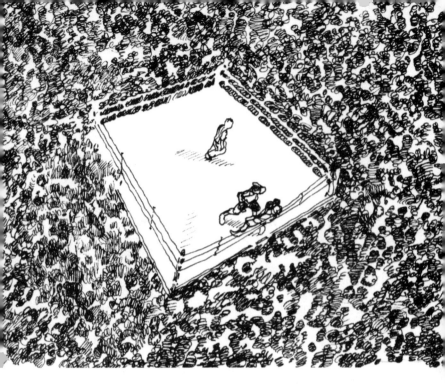

That was a bigger audience than had watched the first moon landing in 1969. The two boxers slugged it out for fifteen punishing rounds. Ali danced, but perhaps not as quickly as before. Frazier battered Ali, and even knocked him down. After the fight was over, the judges said Frazier had won. It was the first loss of Muhammad Ali's pro boxing career.

Soon after, however, Ali won a different sort of fight. The US Supreme Court heard his appeal and accepted his reasons for refusing the draft. They erased his conviction! He stood up for what he believed, and others came to believe the same thing.

But he was still not the world heavyweight champion. In 1974, he got his revenge on Frazier, winning a twelve-round decision. However, Frazier was not the champ by then; he had already lost the title to George Foreman. To become champion again, Ali would have to win the championship from Foreman.

Meanwhile, millions in Africa loved Ali as a black Muslim champion. So, in late 1974, Mobutu Sese Seko, the leader of the African nation of Zaire,

GEORGE FOREMAN

WORLD HEAVYWEIGHT CHAMPIONSHIP
DIRECT FROM KINSHASA, ZAIRE · TUESDAY, SEPTEMBER 24
15 ROUNDS

GEORGE FOREMAN VS MUHAMMAD ALI

offered Ali and Foreman $5 million each to have their heavyweight championship fight in his country. The two boxers accepted and headed to Zaire for a fight called the Rumble in the Jungle. Ali debuted a new poem for this fight:

> *I have wrestled with an alligator,*
> *I have tussled with a whale.*
> *I have handcuffed lightning,*
> *and put thunder in jail. . . .*
> *Only last week, I hospitalized a brick.*
> *I'm so mean I made medicine sick.*

In Zaire, huge crowds followed Ali wherever he went. They would chant, "Ali, *bomaye*, Ali, *bomaye*!" That meant "Ali, kill him!" They wanted their hero to beat young George Foreman and become champ again. Ali was in Zaire for more than a month before the fight. He traveled the country and spoke to thousands of people. He told reporters traveling with him from America, "I want to uplift my brothers sleeping on concrete floors, black people living on welfare,

black people who can't eat, black people who have no future. I want to win [back] my title and help a lot of people." His words during this trip to Africa played a big part in cementing his role as a world celebrity.

His actions in the ring made him a boxing legend . . . again.

HOWARD COSELL

AT RINGSIDE FOR THE FIGHT IN ZAIRE WAS A MAN WHO WAS—AT THE TIME—ALMOST AS FAMOUS IN AMERICA AS ALI. ABC SPORTS ANNOUNCER HOWARD COSELL HAD A DISTINCTIVE VOICE, HE WAS LOUD, HE USED BIG WORDS, AND HE WAS VERY SURE OF HIMSELF. COSELL WAS BOTH LOVED AND HATED. HE WAS ONCE VOTED AS THE FAVORITE AND THE LEAST FAVORITE TV SPORTS VOICE IN THE COUNTRY IN THE SAME YEAR!

AS A TV ANNOUNCER, COSELL OFTEN DESCRIBED BOXING MATCHES, INCLUDING MANY OF ALI'S BIGGEST FIGHTS. HIS HUGE EGO AND PERSONALITY WERE A MATCH FOR ALI'S.

THEIR INTERVIEWS WERE ALWAYS ENTERTAINING.
COSELL TRIED TO CHALLENGE ALI, WHILE ALI
MADE FUN OF THE BROADCASTER'S HAIR OR HIS
PARTICULAR WAY OF SPEAKING.

COSELL ANNOUNCED BOXING MATCHES FOR
MANY YEARS, HAD SEVERAL SPORTS INTERVIEW
SHOWS, AND WAS PART OF ABC'S *MONDAY NIGHT
FOOTBALL* FROM 1970-1984. HIS MOST FAMOUS
SAYING WAS "I TELL IT LIKE IT IS."

In boxing history, only a few men had ever won back a championship title they had lost. On October 30, 1974, Muhammad Ali did. Some reports say that more than one billion people watched the Rumble in the Jungle. Foreman was younger, bigger, and stronger than Ali. Most people thought Ali would lose the fight. To take on Foreman, Ali came up with a plan he called "rope-a-dope." As soon as the fight began, he let Foreman hit him again and again while Ali leaned back against the ropes. But the blows landed mostly on Ali's arms. They hurt, but they didn't slow Ali down. Eventually, Foreman tired in the African heat of the outdoor soccer stadium where the match was held, and Ali pounced. In the eighth round, he stunned Foreman with a huge right-handed blow. The champion was out . . . and Ali was the king of the world again.

Chapter 7
Thrilla in Manila

By the mid-1970s, Muhammad Ali was perhaps the most famous person in the world.

More than anything, fans wanted to see a third fight between Ali and Joe Frazier.

On October 1, 1975, the two veteran fighters met in the capital of the Philippines. The event was called the Thrilla in Manila.

Ali and Frazier knew each other very well. They battled toe-to-toe for round after round. Each man gave and received awful shots to the head and body. Neither gave in until finally, Frazier had had enough. He could not come out to fight the fifteenth round. Ali won and remained champion. But he had taken a terrible pounding.

In the dressing room afterward, he said, "It was the closest thing to dying."

Some people hoped that Ali would stop fighting after the Manila bout. He had taken a lot of punishment for many years. But Ali kept boxing. He won six more fights, but he was getting hit more and more. He was not as quick as he had once been and could not avoid all the punches. Doctors and others worried that he would be permanently injured.

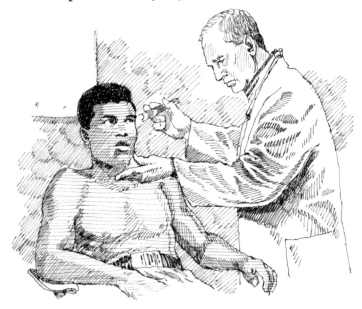

In February 1978, Ali lost his title again. In one of the biggest boxing upsets ever, twenty-four-year-old Leon Spinks beat Ali in Las Vegas. But the old champion had one more comeback in him. Later that same year, Ali, then almost thirty-seven years old, won the title back from Spinks. He became the first person ever to win the heavyweight title *three* times.

By this time, Ali had divorced Khalilah and married Veronica Porsche, whom he had met in 1975. He had two more children with Veronica,

daughters Hana and Laila. (Ali also has two other daughters, Miya and Khaliah, with women who were not his wives.) With his expanding family, Ali finally began to see that it was time to stop fighting. He retired in 1979, but he came back to fight a pair of embarrassing losses. He was beaten easily by fighters he would have defeated in his prime. He was fighting just to make money, not to earn a title. During this time, he continued to move away from the separatist views of the old Nation of Islam. He came to follow simply Islam itself. In 1981, he retired from boxing for good.

In 1984, Ali faced a new and more difficult battle, far from the ring. He was diagnosed with Parkinson's disease, which affects the central nervous system. His brain was not making the right connections to some of his muscles anymore, and this affected his ability to move properly. He trembled and had trouble speaking and walking. Over time, his face became "frozen," or without expression.

LAILA ALI, BOXER

LAILA ALI FOLLOWED HER FATHER'S PATH TO THE BOXING RING, BECOMING ONE OF THE MOST SUCCESSFUL FEMALE FIGHTERS EVER.

IN 1999, SHE HAD HER FIRST FIGHT AND WON BY KNOCKOUT. SHE WOULD GO ON TO WIN TWENTY-FOUR PROFESSIONAL FIGHTS, TWENTY-ONE OF THEM BY KNOCKING OUT HER OPPONENT. LAILA CAPTURED THE SUPER MIDDLEWEIGHT WORLD CHAMPIONSHIP. THOUGH HER FATHER DID NOT SUPPORT HER BOXING CAREER AT FIRST, HE LATER BECAME VERY PROUD OF HER ACCOMPLISHMENTS.

LAILA RETIRED FROM BOXING IN 2007. THAT SAME YEAR, SHE APPEARED ON TV'S *DANCING WITH THE STARS* AND MADE THE FINALS. SHE HAS APPEARED AS A SPOKESPERSON FOR FITNESS AND BEAUTY PRODUCTS, BUT IS STILL MOSTLY KNOWN FOR HER SUCCESS IN THE BOXING RING.

Many doctors felt that being hit in the head so many times during his long boxing career had caused his Parkinson's disease. Ali did not want people's pity. Though no longer the same man, he knew that his fame could still make a difference in the world. He wanted to help other people and spread a message of peace.

Sick or not, Muhammad Ali still had fight in him.

Chapter 8
After Boxing

In 1986, Ali's marriage to Veronica ended.
He had met an old friend from Louisville named
Lonnie Williams. They married in 1986, and she
became a great help to him in his life after boxing.
In 1991, they adopted a son, Asaad, who grew up

to be a college baseball star. In all, Ali has nine children.

Family was very important to Ali. Lonnie's mother had been one of Odessa Clay's best friends, and Ali remained very close to his mother until her death in 1994. Cassius Clay Sr. had died in 1990, long after leaving the family. He and his son had spoken occasionally, but Ali was never as close to his father as he was to Odessa.

Because of his illness, talking and moving became harder and harder, but Ali's charm continued to make him a great communicator. He traveled the world in the 1990s, sharing a message of peace and trying to help poor and hungry people. His fame allowed him to travel to countries where Americans are not usually welcome. In 1990, he went to Iraq and arranged for fifteen American hostages to be released.

They had been held by Iraqi leader Saddam
Hussein in an effort to prevent the United States
from attacking his country. Ali also took medical
supplies to Cuba when that country faced a crisis.
When the black South African leader Nelson
Mandela was released from prison in 1990, Ali
met him soon after.

One of the greatest moments in Ali's life after boxing came in 1996, when he was chosen to light the torch to open the Summer Olympics in Atlanta. The selection of Ali was a well-kept secret. Only a handful of people knew about it before the magic moment when the Champ once again stepped in front of the world. Millions watched as he held the torch steady with his right hand, while his left hand trembled and his face remained a mask. It was an amazing moment in modern Olympic history.

The United Nations named Ali a Messenger of Peace in 1998. That same year, *The Ring* magazine named him the greatest heavyweight boxer of all time. In 1999, as the twentieth century ended, many media groups looked back on the previous one hundred years. *Sports Illustrated*, ESPN, the Associated Press, and the BBC all named Muhammad Ali as one of the greatest athletes of the twentieth century.

In 2001, Islamic terrorists commandeered passenger planes and attacked the United States

on September 11. Many people blamed all of
Islam for the attacks. Ali spoke out for his faith
and against the terrorists. "Islam is not a killer
religion," he said after visiting the site of the
attacks on New York City. "Islam means peace."
He said that he believed the people who had
committed those crimes did not follow Islam.

November 2005 was a big month for Ali
and his family. First, President George W. Bush
awarded Ali the Presidential Medal of Freedom.

That is the highest honor the United States can give to a person who is not in the military. The award showed how much things had changed. Almost forty years earlier, the government had arrested Ali. Now it was honoring him.

Later that month, the Muhammad Ali Center opened in Louisville, Kentucky. The center teaches people about character, peace, and respect. A large museum at the site tells the story of Ali's amazing life and career.

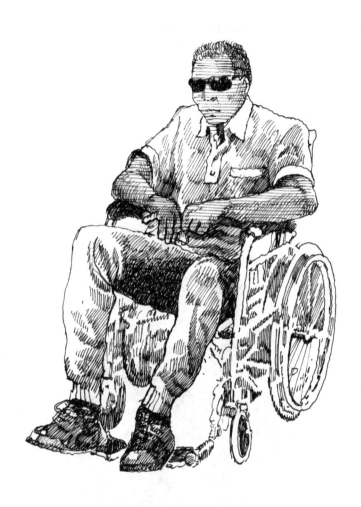

Muhammad Ali's battle with Parkinson's continued. By the early 2000s, he could not smile or talk. He needed help standing and walking.

He made occasional appearances, such as when Barack Obama was sworn in as president in 2009. But in 2016, he developed a serious infection. His weakened body could not win this final fight.

With his family around him, he died in a hospital in Phoenix, Arizona.

Though he is gone, he remains "The Greatest." People remember his courage in the ring, but they value his spirit even more. They admire how he stuck to his beliefs no matter what, and that he used his worldwide fame to try to help millions of people.

Back in 1975, he was asked by a reporter how he would like to be remembered. He said he wanted to be remembered "as a black man who won the heavyweight title and . . . who treated everyone right. As a man who never looked down on those who looked up to him and who helped as many of his people as he could. . . . As a man who tried to unite his people through the faith of Islam."

Most people will remember him as "The Greatest."

TIMELINE OF MUHAMMAD ALI'S LIFE

1942	Born as Cassius Clay in Louisville, Kentucky
1954	Meets Joe Martin and begins to box
1959	Wins Golden Gloves, first major championship
1960	Wins Olympic gold medal in light-heavyweight class
1964	Defeats Sonny Liston to become world heavyweight champion Joins Nation of Islam Changes name to Muhammad Ali
1967	Arrested for refusing to join the army
1970	Returns to boxing after three years off
1971	Loses first fight to Joe Frazier, the Fight of the Century
1974	Defeats George Foreman in Zaire to regain heavyweight title
1975	Defeats Joe Frazier in the Thrilla in Manila
1978	Loses to Leon Spinks Defeats Spinks to again regain title
1981	Retires from boxing for good
1984	Diagnosed with Parkinson's disease
1998	Named Messenger of Peace by United Nations
1999	Named one of the greatest athletes of the century by many sports groups
2005	Awarded Presidential Medal of Freedom Muhammad Ali Center opens in Louisville
2016	Dies in Phoenix, Arizona

TIMELINE OF THE WORLD

World War II ends	1945
Vietnam War begins	1950s
John Glenn becomes the first American to orbit the Earth	1962
Martin Luther King Jr. leads the March on Washington President John F. Kennedy is assassinated in Dallas	1963
President Johnson signs the landmark Civil Rights Act	1964
Martin Luther King Jr. is assassinated in Memphis	1968
Vietnam War ends	1975
Berlin Wall falls in Germany	1989
Gulf War begins as US-led force kicks Iraq out of Kuwait	1990
South Africa ends the system separating blacks and whites	1991
Tiger Woods becomes the first black golfer to win the Masters	1997
Terrorists attack the United States on September 11, destroying the World Trade Center and damaging the Pentagon	2001
America invades Iraq	2003
Barack Obama becomes the first African American to be elected US president	2008
London hosts the Summer Olympic Games	2012
Pope Francis I becomes the first person from South America to be elected to the office	2013

BIBLIOGRAPHY

* Buckley, James Jr. **Muhammad Ali**. Milwaukee: World Almanac Library, 2004.

Gorn, Elliott, ed. **Muhammad Ali: The People's Champ**. Champaign, IL: University of Illinois, 1995.

Hauser, Thomas. **Muhammad Ali: His Life and Times**. New York: Simon & Schuster, 1992.

* Helfand, Lewis. **Muhammad Ali: The King of the Ring**. New Delhi: Campfire, 2011.

* Myers, Walter Dean. **The Greatest: Muhammad Ali**. New York: Scholastic, 2001.

* Timblin, Stephen. **Muhammad Ali: King of the Ring**. New York: Sterling Publishing, 2010.

Maraniss, David. **Rome 1960: The Olympics That Changed the World**. New York: Simon & Schuster, 2008.

* Books for young readers

Official Site
www.ali.com
Muhammad Ali and his family have an official website. It has a long biography, photos from his life, and news on his travels.